本教材获美国2009"月光"国际少年图书奖铜奖

Moonbeam Children's Book Awards
2009"月光"国际少年图书奖颁奖辞

Here is an excellent bilingual tool for helping English-speaking children with the difficult task of learning Chinese language. Recognizing that all children learn in different ways and that holding their attention can be difficult, Dr. Zhou uses a combination of bright and bold illustrations, clever rhymes on topics kids enjoy, music, and even animated cartoons on an included DVD to give children all the tools they need to learn Chinese–and have fun doing it.

Jim Barnes, Awards Director

Victorian Multicultural Awards for Excellence 2009
Dr. Xiaokang Zhou–Education
2009维多利亚州多元文化杰出贡献奖颁奖辞
周晓康博士——教育

Dr. Xiaokang Zhou arrived in Australia in 1989 as an international student. By 1999, Xiaokang had gained a doctorate in Linguistics, a qualification as a Mandarin-English translator and a Graduate Diploma in Education. The following year she began her career in education, teaching ESL and LOTE at Peninsula School, Mt Eliza. She has written and published almost 300 rhymes/songs to help students learn Chinese easily and more effectively—a project that has earned her wide recognition as an innovative and passionate teacher.

Victorian Multicultural Commission, Australia

专家学者推荐

周晓康博士多年来从事语言教学工作,积累了丰富的第二语言教学经验。《晓康歌谣学汉语》是她在教学中用心编写的辅助教学工具,用学生喜闻乐见的方式进行汉语教学,很受学生欢迎。我很欣赏她的创造精神,她的智慧,她的热情,她的别出心裁和独辟蹊径。

崔希亮博士,北京语言大学教授、校长,世界汉语教学学会副会长

板起面孔教汉语是我国对外汉语教学存在的问题之一。大家都说要增强教材的趣味性,可是怎样增强?《晓康歌谣学汉语》开辟了一条新路,这条新路的最大特点就是把歌谣的形式和汉语教学有机地结合起来,通过提高学生的学习兴趣和动力,让学生在寓教于乐中学会汉语。这套书确实是个百宝箱:语言的,社会的,自然的,人文的,方方面面,尽在其中。令我更为叹服的是把一些语法难点也编入歌谣,学生可以通过歌唱、表演等方式轻易达到熟练掌握,真正做到了使语法学习化难为易。

吕必松教授,原北京语言学院院长,原国家汉办主任

因某个特殊的机缘,我有幸提前读到了《晓康歌谣学汉语》的初稿,如获至宝,当即请求她同意在我主编的《新金山教育周报》上连载。今年初还请晓康老师到我们新金山中文学校用她创作的这套教材亲自执教,美其名曰"种一块试验田"。连载大获好评,试验田大获丰收,晓康歌谣唱响了校园内外。为此,我要向晓康老师表示衷心的感谢和祝贺。

孙浩良,澳大利亚新金山中文学校创办人

Dr. Zhou's Rhymes for Learning Chinese could be an ideal resource material used in conjunction with other grammar-focused textbooks to promote performance-based language learning or used for Chinese Cultural Day or Open Day.

I highly recommend this series to anyone who teaches non-Chinese speaking background learners but find it difficult to motivate their learners and engage them to learn this challenging but also very rewarding language.

Dr. Guanxin Ren, Camberwell Grammar School, Melbourne, Australia

Dr. Zhou's Rhymes For Learning Chinese

中英双语视听版

晓康歌谣学汉语

第1集
Book 1

【澳】周晓康　著
【澳】周晓康　T. Gourdon　译

By Dr. Xiaokang Zhou
Translated by Dr. Xiaokang Zhou & T. Gourdon

北京大学出版社

图书在版编目(CIP)数据

晓康歌谣学汉语.第1集/(澳)周晓康著；X. Zhou & T. Gourdon 译. —北京：北京大学出版社，2009.5
ISBN 978-7-301-15005-4

Ⅰ.晓… Ⅱ.周… Ⅲ.汉语-对外汉语教学-教材 Ⅳ.H195.4

中国版本图书馆CIP数据核字(2009)第034324号

欢迎访问《晓康歌谣学汉语》的博客：http://blog.sina.com.cn/xkgy，更多精彩，与您分享！

书　　　　名	：晓康歌谣学汉语 第1集
著作责任者	：〔澳〕周晓康 著　X. Zhou & T. Gourdon 译
责 任 编 辑	：旷书文 shanekuang@126.com
标 准 书 号	：ISBN 978-7-301-15005-4/H·2218
出 版 发 行	：北京大学出版社
地　　　　址	：北京市海淀区成府路205号 100871
网　　　　址	：http://www.pup.cn　新浪官方微博@：北京大学出版社
电 子 信 箱	：zpup@pup.pku.edu.cn
电　　　　话	：邮购部 62752015　发行部 62750672　编辑部 62753374　出版部 62754962
印 刷 者	：北京中科印刷有限公司
经 销 者	：新华书店
	889毫米×1194毫米　大16开本　3.5印张　110千字
	2009年5月第1版　2017年5月第5次印刷
定　　　　价	：69.00元（附1张DVD、1张MP3）

未经许可，不得以任何方式复制或抄袭本书之部分或全部内容。
版权所有，侵权必究
举报电话：010-62752024　电子信箱：fd@pup.pku.edu.cn

序一　赵世开　　1
Preface I　Shikai Zhao

序二　哈伟　　3
Preface II　Wei Ha

自序　周晓康　5
Author's Preface　Xiaokang Zhou

1. 字母歌　1
The Chinese Alphabet Song

2. 笔画歌　2
The Character Stroke Song

3. 四声歌　3
The Four Tones Song

4. 山水歌　4
Mountains and Water

5. 林火歌　5
Forests and Fire

6. 人口歌　6
The Population Song

7. 大好河山　7
Grand Rivers and Mountains

8. 你好！　8
Hello!

9. 问候歌　9
The Greeting Song

10. 我你他　10
I You and He

11. 上课　11
The Lesson Song

12. 数字歌　12
The Number Song

13. 顺口溜　14
A Tongue Twister

14. 拍手歌　15
The Hand-Clapping Song

15. 你是谁? **17**
Who are You?

16. 谁啊? **18**
Who is It?

17. 你几岁? **20**
How Old are You?

18. 文具歌 **21**
The Stationery Song

19. 我的学习用品 **22**
My Stationery

20. 教室歌 **23**
Classroom Objects

21. 这是谁的书? **25**
Whose Book is This?

22. 你们知道不知道? **27**
Do You Know or Not?

23. 游戏歌 **28**
Let's Play the Game

24. 家人歌 **29**
The Family Song

25. 我爱爸爸和妈妈 **30**
I Love Dad and Mum

中文词汇表(简繁对照) **32**
英文词汇表(简繁对照) **36**
《晓康歌谣学汉语》总目录 **41**
作者简介 **43**
编后记 **44**

序 一

本书著者周晓康博士曾给我留下很深刻的印象。她学习和工作都非常勤奋。上个世纪八十年代,她在北京大学英语系攻读博士学位时,听了很多中文系的课,这使得她对汉语有了系统的科学的认识。在英文系的学生中,她的这一优点显得特别突出。后来她到澳大利亚继续攻读博士学位,又听了很多现代理论语言学的课,完成了现代汉语句子生成的系统功能计算语言学模式。作为一名语言学学者,她具有雄厚的理论基础,令人敬佩。

出乎我意料的是:她在澳大利亚取得博士学位后,勇敢地涉足中小学的汉语作为第二语言的教学,而且她是全身心地投入,这是很难得的。在语言学界,理论语言学和应用语言学这二者之间似乎隔了一堵墙。周晓康能跨越这两个领域,这在语言学界不多见。这是一种突破。这一突破能使得她在两方面都相互促进,这也就能使她在两方面都做得更出色。本书就是一个例证。

我认为《晓康歌谣学汉语》是一套很好的对外汉语教材。它的对象是非母语背景学习汉语的中小学生。这个年龄段的学生是学习外语最重要的时期,也就是奠定基础的时期。根据我的经验,这个时期背诵的课文往往能长久地记住。我深信这套书里的歌谣会一直留在学生的记忆里。采用歌谣加强外语学习的印象是很有效的方法。如今我虽已八十多岁,仍能记得小时候在上海学的"来叫come,去叫go,二十四叫twenty four"这样的顺口溜。可见,背诵是学习语言的一条有效途径。更何况,这套歌谣中的所有歌曲都制作成了精彩而优美的卡拉OK动画。多媒体技术的应用,无疑使得汉语学习更加妙趣横生。中国有句老话:"熟读唐诗三百首,不会作诗也会吟",这一方法应该继承下来。周晓康正是这样做的。在这里我想重复上面说过的周晓康突破了中文系和外文系的界限,突破了理论和应用的界限,她还把中国和西方的传统和特点结合了起来,这是十分难得的,这也是我最欣赏和推崇的。可惜我自己都没有做到。

由于周晓康具有坚实的语言学理论的基础,在这本歌谣里我们可以看出她别具匠心地去处理汉语的一些特点。首先关于口语和书面语的关系,将《字母歌》作为第一首歌谣,完全符合"先听说,后读写"的语言学习顺序,即从口语到书面语的渐进过程。其次,关于语言和文字的关系,汉字具有它独特的性质,跟西方的拼音文字是不同的。其中的笔画是它的基本要素,所以歌谣的第二首就是《笔画歌》,这的确是抓住了要点。又例如汉语的语音结构中,声调是一大特点。作者把《四声歌》排在第三课,这真是精彩的处理。

这套歌谣是在教学实践中形成的。一般教材的编写者和教学者不是同一个人。记得 **M.A.K. Halliday** 曾经说过,教材编写者是学者,教师是演员。周晓康在这方面又将学者和演员结合在一起。我想这套教材一定能非常适用。

作为一个读者,我十分欣赏这套歌谣。为此我向编者致以敬意和祝贺,也愿意热情地向大家推荐这套出色的教材。

赵世开
2008年1月2日于北京方庄寓所

Preface I

Shikai Zhao

I have been deeply impressed with Dr. Xiaokang Zhou, the author of this book of rhymes. She was very diligent in her studies and work. In the 1980's, when she was studying for a Ph. D. degree at the English Department of Beijing University, she audited many courses offered by the Chinese Department. As a result, she was able to gain a systematic knowledge of the science of philology of the Chinese language. Later, when she went to Australia to continue her doctorate studies, she took many courses on modern linguistic theories in the Department of Linguistics of The University of Melbourne, and was able to accomplish a computational linguistic model for sentence generation based on the systemic-functional analysis of the sentence structures of modern Chinese. Thus, she has admirably laid down a solid academic foundation as a scholar of philology.

It was to my surprise that after she obtained the doctorate degree in Australia, she ventured to enter the profession of teaching Chinese as a second language to students of secondary schools. Much to her credit, she applied herself to the new career with dedication. There seems to exist a barrier between the theory and the practice of linguistics. It is therefore remarkable for Dr. Zhou to overcome this barrier and to achieve a breakthrough—a breakthrough that allows her to bring the two fields together to their mutual benefit and thereby make a significant contribution of her own in both fields. It is also remarkable that she has been able to blend together different traditions and features of the Chinese and Western cultures. This achievement has earned my deep appreciation and respect. *Dr. Zhou's Rhymes* exemplifies that effort.

In my view, *Dr. Zhou's Rhymes* is an excellent supplementary material for the teaching of Chinese to non-Chinese students. It is targeted at students of primary and secondary schools who have no Chinese background. This group of students is at a critical age of mastering any foreign language — a period for them to lay the foundation of learning the language. I know from my own experience that many lessons learned by rote at the young age are likely to be retained in the memory for a long time. I am therefore convinced that the rhymes contained in this book will be long remembered by students.

The book of rhymes was gradually compiled in the course of the author's teaching career. An author of teaching material is usually not one and the same person as a teacher. It is said by M. A. K. Halliday that the author is a scholar, while the teacher is an actor. Dr. Xiaokang Zhou is a scholar as well as a teacher.

As a reader, I very much appreciate and enjoy this book of rhymes. Accordingly, I extend to the author my best wishes and congratulations and take great pleasure in recommending to the public this outstanding teaching material.

January 2, 2008
Fangzhuang, Beijing

序 二

《晓康歌谣学汉语》是用来进行汉语教学,特别是对外汉语教学的歌谣,是周晓康博士近几年汉语教学的成果。

歌谣是韵文最常见的一种形式,这种韵文形式最能反映汉语的特点。以韵文的形式进行识字教育和语言教学,已经有几千年的历史了。从周宣王时的《史籀篇》到南北朝时的《千字文》,再到宋朝的《百家姓》和《三字经》,韵文一直都是学习汉语的重要工具。现代语言学大师赵元任先生在方言研究和语言教学中也编写过一些歌谣。

《晓康歌谣学汉语》一共有两百多首,这些歌谣包括了汉语教学的方方面面,既可以和汉语教科书配套使用,也可以配合任何形式的汉语教学。这套歌谣集有这样几个特点:

一、系统全面,涵盖面广。歌谣中既有字音的识别和汉字的笔画顺序,也有常见的话题和一些基本的文化知识。歌谣在这里不仅仅是一种教学手段,更是一种对教材的补充。

二、短小精悍,朗朗上口。使用歌谣教学既能使学生通过歌谣来感受汉语特有的韵律,又能使学生通过歌谣记住所学的知识,因此歌谣必须做到节奏明快,朗朗上口。比如《放风筝》这一首:"放风筝,放风筝,风筝飞上天;随风飘呀飘,赛过活神仙。"

三、针对性。这些歌谣跟市面上流行的汉语儿歌不同,在语言和文化上都具有很强的针对性,是专门为非汉语和汉文化背景的学生编写的,因此不仅英汉对照,同时在韵文格式上也参考了英文中韵文的习惯,优美的英文翻译,也是学生学习英语的好素材。

四、欣赏性和娱乐性。这套教材的另外一大亮点是,请专业音乐和动画人士做了丰富多样的电子音乐伴奏和活泼可爱的卡通动画,使用者可以一边享受美妙的音画艺术一边卡拉OK朗诵和演唱,使得中文学习真正成为一种精神愉悦和享受。

五、互动性。这套教材还在网络上开设了博客,提供了跟教材相关的教学提示、视频、教学手记、学生习作等资源,这能让使用者真切感受教学实况,并能与作者在线交流互动,别有趣味。

周晓康博士是我在北京大学的同学。她曾在英语系攻读博士学位,专攻西方语言学,同时对汉语也颇有研究。我那时在北大中文系教现代汉语,同时攻读现代汉语的研究生学位。我们在北大时虽然不认识,但是我们都曾在同一个课堂里听过朱德熙先生、叶蜚声先生、徐通锵先生和陆俭明先生的课。真正结识周晓康博士还是到了澳洲以后,说起来也已经快20年了。

王力先生曾特别提倡龙虫并雕,陆俭明先生在谈到对外汉语教师的素质时,也特别强调要有专家来研究对外汉语教学,只有这样才能提高对外汉语教学的水平。在国外教外国人学习汉语,不仅需要汉语教师观念的转变,更需要应对各种情况的能力。周晓康博士的《晓康歌谣学汉语》无疑是这方面的一个有益尝试,我们真心希望更多的专家学者投身于对外汉语教学中来。

哈伟
2007年10月于墨尔本

Preface II
Wei Ha

Dr. Zhou's Rhymes presents a collection of rhymes in Chinese useful for the teaching of the Chinese language, particularly to non-Chinese students. The rhymes are composed by Dr. Xiaokang Zhou on the basis of her practical experiences in teaching Chinese in recent years.

Rhyme is a most common form of rhythmic verses. The rhyming form can be used to its best advantage in the Chinese language. In the history of China, it has been in use for literacy education and language teaching for thousands of years. Starting from the *Shi Zhou Pian* in the reign of King Xuan of Zhou Dynasty, to the *Verse of Thousand Characters* in the epoch of Southern and Northern Dynasties, and to the *Book of Family Names* and the *Trimetrical Classic* of Song Dynasty, a series of primers have resorted to the form of rhyme as a way of teaching and learning Chinese.

Dr. Zhou's Rhymes contains more than two hundred verses. The rhymes cover all aspects of the Chinese language pedagogy. They can be useful not only as a supplement to existing textbooks, such as the *Ni Hao* series, but also as a complement to any other method of teaching and learning Chinese. This book of rhymes is marked by the following distinct features.

1. It is systematic and has a broad coverage. The rhymes not only illustrate the tonal differentiation in pronunciation and the strokes system in writing (that are peculiar to the Chinese language), but also cover a wide range of topics that are of common interest or involve basic cultural knowledge.

2. The rhymes are short, vibrant and fit for singing aloud. Their use enables students to appreciate the peculiar rhythms of the Chinese language, while reinforcing their memory of the knowledge imparted by the lessons. For this purpose, the rhymes have to be rhythmic and melodious.

3. The rhymes are designed for a specific purpose, but have a wider field of application. They are primarily intended for the use of learning Chinese by students who have no Chinese background. To them, the excellent English translation of the verses offers an additional benefit for their learning of English.

As Master Wang Li advocated, a sculpturer should be adept at carving a dragon as well as an insect. Speaking of the qualifications of instructors teaching Chinese to foreigners, professor Lu Jian-Ming has likewise emphasized the need for experts to do research on the methodology of teaching so as to enhance the level of instruction in this specialized field. It behooves teachers of Chinese outside China not only to make necessary adjustments in their method of instruction, but also to be able to cope with the different environments of teaching. The book *Dr. Zhou's Rhymes* is undoubtedly a positive attempt to achieving this objective. We sincerely hope that more and more experts and scholars will engage themselves in the work of promoting the theory and practice of teaching Chinese to foreigners.

October, 2007

自序

我自上个世纪九十年代获墨尔本大学语言学博士学位,到本世纪初转入教育领域,从抽象的理论语言学研究,转向应用语言学的最具体的汉语教学实践,至今竟也快十个年头了!这当中从理念到方法,从对象到语料都是"天翻地复"的变化。

来澳洲之前,我在中国杭州大学(今浙江大学)教过对外汉语。但毕竟那时的教学对象都是来自美国的大学生、研究生,教的内容以词法、语法分析为主,没什么课堂纪律问题,所以感觉是"驾轻就熟"、"游刃有余"。而现在这里面对的是从7年级到12年级的中学生,教学又是以"娱乐"为主,必须"生动活泼",方能"立竿见影"。对我们这些母语非英语的老师来说,谈何容易!

这些年来,我在澳洲进行汉语教学的实践中思考最多、挑战最大的就是如何吸引学生的注意力,提高他们对学汉语的兴趣和积极性。人人都说汉语难:四声难辨,汉字难写,句子难记。关键是要化难为易,化繁为简,化苦为乐。在我的各种摸索和尝试中,最有效、最能让学生接受的就是我根据教材内容撰写的歌谣。为了让学生更好地掌握课文的词汇和句型及相关的文化背景知识,我把一些生词和句子编写成一首又一首的歌谣,穿插在课文中教,发现效果非常好,学生们学唱歌谣的兴趣和积极性非常高,几乎个个都能把这些歌谣背得滚瓜烂熟,就连那些平时最吵闹、最调皮、最懒散的学生也都会跟上来背得头头是道,学习效率普遍提高。这真让我感到莫大的欣慰和激动!

激动之余,2007年7月初,我在墨尔本召开的第13届全澳中文教师年会上作了一个报告,介绍了我这几年用歌谣教学的心得体会,并当场演示了我在课堂上用过的二十来首歌谣。真没想到,我的报告会场座无虚席,从原先限制的最多不得超过30人,增至54人,连环绕教室一周的桌子上都坐满了人!有的老师还把我的报告从头到尾都录了像,把每首在屏幕上出现的歌谣都拍了照带回去。会后,大家争先恐后地向我索取那几首歌谣,很多老师建议我快点出书。看到老师们这么需要这样的教学资料,我深受鼓舞和激励! 2008年12月,我应邀参加了在北京举行的第九届国际汉语教学研讨会,会上就《晓康歌谣学汉语》做了一个教学演示,演示现场真可以用"爆满"两字来形容。很多老师都对这种教学形式和方法极感兴趣。此届大会上,我的演示获得了"国际汉语教学创新示范课奖",得到了同行的肯定和赞赏,这不能不让我又一次深受激励和鼓舞!

虽说多年来国内出版的汉语儿歌、童谣不少,但它们的读者大多是以汉语为母语的人群,其中的词汇和句型对非汉语背景的外国学生有一定难度,且文化背景也大相径庭。而我的这套歌谣集,完全是为海外学汉语的非母语背景学生所编写。相比之下,它具有以下几个明显的特征:

1. 每首歌谣内容与学生所学课文密切相关,相辅相成,互为补充,适合任何以话题形式编写的课本,既可用作辅助教材,也可像其他儿歌、童谣那样单独使用;

2. 语言浅显朴素,简明易懂,生动活泼,押韵对称,朗朗上口,结构短小精悍,关键词和句型重现率高,反复吟诵,牢记不忘;

3. 形式多样,有对话、猜谜、游戏、顺口溜等,适用双人或小组表演,能促进口头交流,互动互学;

4. 每一首中文歌谣都编译成了地道的、风趣幽默的英文韵文,有利于提高学生的英文水平;

5. 本教材的最大亮点是每一首歌谣都配上了优美动听的曲调,谱曲中有不少旋律取自于学生们所熟悉的中英文歌曲,并请专业音乐和动画人士做成动画卡拉OK,伴奏丰富多彩,卡通活泼有趣,歌声甜润迷人,学生可以跟着卡拉OK朗诵和演唱,同时培养语感和乐感,使语言学习真正成为一种享受!

有言道:"实践是检验真理的标准"。我在2007年对我校不同年级的汉语非母语背景学生做的问卷调查中得到的反馈几乎百分之百是肯定与赞赏的。大家一致认为通过演唱歌谣使汉语学习变得轻松容易多了,很多以前怎么也记不住的单词和句子现在都能"自动"地从脑中跳出来,而且是牢牢地"刻"在了脑中,"挥之不去",那是得益于歌谣中的"catchy tunes"(扣人心弦的曲调/旋律)和"令人兴奋的节奏感和朗朗上口的韵脚";很多学生表示学了这些歌谣后,大大地提高了对课文中的单词和句型的理解和运用,甚至能帮助他们在考试中"不假思索","脱口而出"!有的学生说,自从学了几首中文歌谣,每星期天天盼着上汉语课;有的学生说每次上完汉语课,总会情不自禁地反复哼着新学的歌,不管校内还是校外,都会听到同学们在唱中文歌,甚至晚上在家里也会哼上几句,真是有点儿"走火入魔","潜移默化",一点儿不夸张! 同时也有很多老师拿着我的歌谣在试用,不论在什么国家教学,用下来的课堂效果都是出奇地好,有的老师甚至开始"依赖"上这套歌谣,又一次让我深感欣慰和鼓舞!音乐无国界,它使学习更快乐,更精彩!

另外,我想就这套教材的体例和配套音像产品作一简单说明:

1. 基于对外汉语教学的特点和我自己的教学体会,本书在歌词的中英对照注释方面,主要采取字面直译,而非逐句翻译。这样做的目的是为了让学生了解每个词语的意义以及在句子中出现的位置,能更直观地反映汉语和英语两种语言的本来面目及其在构词、造句等方面的语义、语序和句法结构的差异,使学生能更好地了解和关注两种语言的区别。老师们在使用本书时,需要就这些现象跟学生讲解汉英两种语言的特点和异同,这样可以举一反三,融会贯通。

2. 英文翻译方面,本书以韵文见长,不拘泥于原文,采取自由灵活的意译和改写,使之在符合原文基本内容的前提下,增加了可读性和趣味性。不仅节奏明快,朗朗上口,而且幽默风趣,生动活泼,给学生一种额外的享受:不仅是学语言,同时也学了该语言的文化和文学。通常还可以结合诗歌翻译技巧教学,开拓视野,扩大词汇量和知识面。

3. 本书配动画DVD光盘和MP3光盘,DVD包括中文朗诵、演唱卡拉OK和英文朗诵动画,MP3光盘包括中文朗诵、演唱,英文朗诵以及中英文生词朗读,这给教学提供了最直观、最具视觉和听觉效果的资源,集语言、美术、音乐、娱乐于一体,使学生不仅能在教室里,而且还能在课后任何场合,包括放学回家,在电脑上或身边随时播放、跟读或跟唱;还可以组织卡拉OK演唱和朗诵比赛! 真正做到寓教于乐,其乐无穷!

最后,我想借此机会,向这些年中所有支持我、鼓励我、协助我的同行、朋友、家长和学生们致以最真诚的谢意。我特别要感谢《你好》作者 Shumang and Paul Fredlein,如果没有这本教科书作蓝本,就不可能有《晓康歌谣》的问世。这里需要特别一提的是,中国语言学界的老前辈,中国社科院语言研究所研究员赵世开教授对本书的出版关怀备至,并为本书起了一个既响亮又亲切的名字。还需要一提的是,我们维州中文教师协会主席,我当年的北大校友哈伟老师凌晨三点给本书作序,不由得让我深受感动! 在此深表感谢!

我衷心期望本书能给每个教汉语的老师、学汉语的同学增添一份新的乐趣! 让我们一起创造一种真正的寓乐于学,轻松活泼的学习气氛,高高兴兴唱儿歌,快快乐乐学汉语!

周晓康
于伊丽莎山庄
2008年2月28日

Author's Preface

Xiaokang Zhou

Over the last few years, I discovered that the biggest challenge in teaching Chinese as a second language is how to keep students' attention and how to interest and inspire them in learning Chinese. Chinese is known to be a very difficult language to learn: the four tones are hard to distinguish; characters are hard to write; and sentences are hard to remember. The key point here is how to make difficult things easy, how to make complicated things simple and how to turn "pain" into "fun". I tried a variety of approaches to simplifying the learning process, such as using flash cards and word games. It turns out that the most effective way of maintaining students' interest, keeping their attention and enabling them to absorb and remember the vocabulary and sentence structures is through reciting and singing rhymes and songs based on the contents of each textbook lesson.

In order to help students to better grasp the vocabulary and sentence structures taught in each lesson, as well as the relevant cultural aspect of each topic, I made use of some newly-learned words, expressions and sentence patterns to compose rhyming verses and use them as a supplementary teaching resource. I found such verses very useful and effective, producing positive results—students were very interested and keen to learn these rhymes, with unbelievable enthusiasm! Almost all students were able to learn these rhymes by heart and recite them fluently, including those who were usually not so attentive and well-disciplined in class! I saw a remarkable improvement in their aptitude and achievement, which made me really happy, deeply touched, and relieved!

In July 2007, excited by such results, I conducted a workshop at the 13th CLTFA National Conference in Melbourne, dwelling on my new experiences and practices in teaching Chinese as a second language through rhymes and songs over the last few years, and giving a power-point presentation of about 20 rhymes and songs I wrote and used in my classes. I was surprised to see the workshop room fully packed with 54 conference delegates, with all seats taken and some of them having to sit on the workbenches and tables, the original number of participants being restricted to 30! Some teachers used their video cameras to record my presentation from the beginning to the end, and others took digital photos of every rhyme that was shown on the screen. After my presentation, most of them asked me for a copy of my rhymes, and many of them urged me to publish the rhymes in book form. This made me feel greatly touched and excited.

Although there have been a number of new publications of Chinese nursery rhymes in China in recent years, they are mainly targeted at first language speakers. Their vocabulary and sentence structures may be too difficult for second language speakers to learn. Besides, because of significant differences in cultural background, it would also be hard for non-native speakers to understand or appreciate them properly.

In contrast, my rhymes are written purely for the teaching of Chinese to students who have no Chinese background at all. These rhymes are closely related to the topics being taught, covering many cultural aspects relevant to students' school and family life. They are extremely simple, rhythmical and symmetrical. Students also find the rhyming repetition stimulating and easy to remember. The rhymes are easily adaptable, encouraging interaction and engaging students in productive learning while enjoying each other's performances.

There is a famous saying in Chinese: "Practice is the best test of truth". In Term 2 of 2007, I carried out a survey among some 60 students in my Years 7-10 CSL classes on this method of teaching and its effects. The feedback was 99.9% positive and appreciative. All but one students indicated that learning through rhymes and songs is much more enjoyable and easier. Many words and sentences that used to elude their memory would now "automatically" spring into their minds and remain firmly implanted. This is due to the catchy tunes and easily recitable rhyming words and rhythms.

Many students responded that after learning the rhymes, they were able to understand the words and sentences better and use them in their own writing with confidence and that the rhymes even helped them do better in their exams, because "the words just follow," "without us trying" and "you know the answer" straight away! Some students said that since learning the rhymes, they began to look forward to the Chinese lessons every day. Others said that every time after the Chinese class, they would keep singing the newly learned songs in and outside of classrooms, even at home after school. Suddenly they found themselves engrossed with these rhymes. That is by no means an exaggeration!

Almost every one of the respondents mentioned that "it is a fun way of learning pinyin and characters." The word "fun" revealed the students' heart-felt fondness of this way of learning.

The responses to the survey remind me of my own experience in learning English. What I remember most is some familiar nursery tunes, such as "Twinkle, twinkle, little star, …" and "Jingle bells, jingle bells, jingle all the way, …" They remain fresh in my memory. It shows the benefit and lasting effect of learning a language through rhymes and songs.

Finally, I would like to take this opportunity to express my sincere thanks to all my friends, colleagues, students and parents for their support, encouragement and assistance in the production of this book. I would especially like to thank Shumang and Paul Fredlein, the authors of the *Nihao* series of textbooks. Without their excellent publication which formed the basis of my work, there would be no *Xiao Kang Ge Yao*.

I would also like to thank Professor Zhao Shikai, a former Research Fellow of the Chinese Academy of Social Science, the former Editor-in-Chief of *Linguistics Abroad*, my old friend and supervisor who guided me into the field of linguistics many years ago. He encouraged me to publish this book and suggested a very special title for it: *Xiao Kang Ge Yao* 晓康歌谣, which contains my name followed by the characters meaning songs and rhymes. My name was originally given by my parents as 小康 (literally meaning "small/little and healthy," also meaning "wealthy" as one term), with the expectation for my generation to enter an era of prosperity. When I grew up, and graduated from primary school, I changed the word xiao 小 "small/ little" to xiao 晓 which means "knowledgeable", implying an ability to know everything, from the ancient to the modern and from the East to the West. I hope the readers of this book, when reciting and singing these simple verses, could share my innermost feelings and retain childhood innocence and dreams.

One person I must give special thanks to is Mr. Ha Wei, my former Beijing University colleague, now the president of the Chinese Language Teachers Association of Victoria, who wrote the preface for this book at 3 a.m.. I was very touched and grateful to him for his support.

Another person I owe my sincere thanks to is Mr. Shing-Yi (S. Y.) Huang, a former official of the United Nations Secretariat and a distant relative on my mother's side, currently living in the USA, for his excellent translation of the two prefaces from Chinese into English, and his encouraging remarks on the content of these rhymes and the art of translation as reflected in the book. I am most grateful to him for his valuable help and advice, as he has long been in retirement, yet remains active in his academic and community work.

The last but not the least person to mention is Tim Gourdon whose genius adaptation of my English translation into rhyming form has added insurmountable pleasure and fun to the reading as well as the learning of these rhymes in English.

I sincerely hope this book of my rhymes will add a new and useful dimension to the teaching/learning of Chinese/English and bring pleasure to every Chinese/English teacher and student who should be praised for their great effort and contribution in promoting the languages and cultures of both Chinese and English.

January 28, 2008

字 母 歌
zì mǔ gē

The Chinese Alphabet Song

b p m f   d t n l

g k h   j q x

zh ch sh   r z c s

a o e   i u ü

这 是 汉 语 字 母 歌，
zhè shì hàn yǔ zì mǔ gē
this is Chinese alphabet song,

人 人 会 唱 人 人 乐。
rén rén huì chàng rén rén lè
every person can sing every person happy

The Chinese Alphabet Song

By Dr. X. Zhou & T. Gourdon

b p m f d t n l   g k h j q x
zh ch sh r   z c s   a o e   i u ü

This is the Chinese Alphabet Song,
We are all happy when we sing along!

笔画歌
The Character Stroke Song

<table>
<tr><td>diǎn
点
dot</td><td>héng
横
horizontal line</td><td>shù
竖
vertical line</td><td>piě
撇
right-ward stroke</td><td>nà
捺，
left-ward stroke</td></tr>
</table>

hái yǒu tí hé gōu
还 有 提 和 勾；
in addition   tick   and   hook

xiě zì shù bǐ huà
写 字 数 笔 画，
write character   count   strokes

yǒng yuǎn jì xīn tóu
永 远 记 心 头。
forever   learn   heart

The Character Stroke Song

By Dr. X. Zhou & T. Gourdon

A dot and a line, horizontal or vertical,
A slanting line to the leftical or rightical,
A tick and a hook, mark in your book.
Then count these basic strokes
When writing a Chinese character,
For *these strokes*
Forever should we remember.

sì shēng gē
四声歌
The Four Tones Song

mā	shì	dì	yī	shēng	má	shì	dì	èr	shēng
妈	是	第	一	声，	麻	是	第	二	声；
mum	is	the 1st		tone	numb	is	the 2nd		tone

mǎ	shì	dì	sān	shēng	mà	shì	dì	sì	shēng
马	是	第	三	声，	骂	是	第	四	声。
horse	is	the 3rd		tone	scold	is	the 4th		tone

hàn	yǔ	yǒu	shēng	diào	yǒng	yuǎn	wàng	bù	liǎo
汉	语	有	声	调，	永	远	忘	不	了！
Chinese		have		tone	forever		never forget		

The Four Tones Song

By Dr. X. Zhou & T. Gourdon

"mā" is "Mum", illustrating Tone Number One,
"má" means "numb", representing Tone Number Two,
"mǎ" is a "horse" with Tone Number Three of course,
"mà" is "to scold" with the Fourth Tone.
Such as when you are told not to be so bold,
Chinese has tones just like a musical note,
We must learn them by rote.

shān shuǐ gē
山 水 歌
Mountains and Water

rì 日 is the sun, yuè 月 is the moon;
(sun) (moon)

Mountain shì 是 shān 山, water shì 是 shuǐ 水;
(is mountain) (is water)

wǒ ài shān, wǒ ài shuǐ
我 爱 山, 我 爱 水;
(I love mountain, I love water)

shān shān shuǐ shuǐ duō me měi
山 山 水 水 多 么 美!
(mountains and rivers so pretty)

Mountains and rivers are so pretty!

rì yuè shān shuǐ

Mountains and Water

By Dr. X. Zhou & T. Gourdon

"rì" is "the sun", "yuè" is "the moon",
"Mountain" is "shān", "Water" is "shuǐ".
I love to climb mountains
with excitement and glee,
And from high above
I love the water I see,
Mountains and rivers are so pretty.

lín huǒ gē
林 火 歌
Forests and Fire

shān shang yǒu shuǐ, shān shang yǒu mù;
山 上 有 水, 山 上 有 木;
on the mountain have water   on the mountain have tree

mù chéng lín, lín zháo huǒ。
木 成 林, 林 着 火。
tree become forest, forest catch fire

rén lái jiù huǒ yòng shuǐ pō,
人 来 救 火 用 水 泼,
person come fight fire   use   water pour

rén rén kāi kǒu xiào hē hē,
人 人 开 口 笑 呵 呵,
every person   open mouth   laugh ho ho ho...

hē hē hē hē hē
呵 呵 呵 呵 呵……
ha ha ha ha ha ....

Forests and Fire

By Dr. X. Zhou & T. Gourdon

There is water on the mountain,
Springing like a fountain;
There are trees on the mountain,
Feeding from the fountain.
The trees grow into forests,
Then the forests catch fire.
As the flames get higher,
People come to pour water on the fire.
When the fire is doused,
Every one laughs with their mouth open wide,
Ha, ha, ha, ha, ha!

人口歌 (rén kǒu gē)
The Population Song

人 (rén / person) 是 (shì / is) person，口 (kǒu / mouth) 是 (shì / is) mouth。

中 (zhōng) 国 (guó) — China 人 (rén) 口 (kǒu) — population 十 (shí) 三 (sān) 亿 (yì) — 1.3 billion，

站 (zhàn / stand) 在 (zài) 一 (yì) 起 (qǐ) — be together 数 (shù) 不 (bù) 清 (qīng) — impossible to count，

全 (quán) 世 (shì) 界 (jiè) — the whole world 第 (dì) 一 (yī) — the first。

赵钱外李周吴郑王冯陈褚卫蒋沈韩杨

The Population Song

By Dr. X. Zhou & T. Gourdon

"rén" is a "person", "kǒu" is "mouth",
"rén" and "kǒu" together form "population".
China's population is 1.3 billion,
Standing together,
This amount is impossible to count.
It's the highest in the world.

7

dà hǎo hé shān
大 好 河 山
Grand Rivers and Mountains

cháng jiāng　huáng　hé　cháng　jiāng　huáng　hé
长 江 , 黄 河 , 长 江 , 黄 河 ,
Yangtze Rive　　Yellow River　　Yangtze River　　Yellow River

dà　yùn　hé　　dà　yùn　hé
大 运 河 , 大 运 河 。
　　Grand Canal　　　　　Grand Canal

huáng shān　tài shān　hé　lú　shān
黄 山 , 泰 山 和 庐 山 ,
Yellow Mountain　Tai Mountain　and　Lu Mountain

xī　hú　tài　hú　dòng tíng hú
西 湖 , 太 湖 , 洞 庭 湖 ,
West Lake　　Tai Lake　　Dongting Lake

dà hǎo hé shān kàn bù wán
大 好 河 山 看 不 完 。
grand rivers and mountains　　impossible to finish

Grand Rivers and Mountains

By Dr. X. Zhou & T. Gourdon

Yangtze River, Yellow River, Yangtze River, Yellow River,
Grand Canal, Grand Canal;
They are definitely not banal.
Yellow Mountains, Tai Mountains, Lu Mountains,
Spectacular in summer rains.
West Lake, Tai Lake, Dongting Lake,
They certainly are not fake.
Grand rivers and mountains,
Timeless and breath-taking,
They keep your mind awake,
Endless and so great!

Hello!

你 好，你 好，老 师 好！
nǐ hǎo　nǐ hǎo　lǎo shī hǎo
Hello　　Hello　　Hello teacher

你 好，你 好，大 伟 好！
nǐ hǎo　nǐ hǎo　dà wěi hǎo
Hello　　Hello　　Hello David

你 早，你 早，兰 兰 早！
nǐ zǎo　nǐ zǎo　lán lan zǎo
good morning　good morning　Lanlan good morning

再 见，再 见，明 天 见！
zài jiàn　zài jiàn　míng tiān jiàn
good bye　good bye　see you tomorrow

Hello!

By Dr. X. Zhou & T. Gourdon

Hello, Hello, Hello Teacher!
It's so good to greetyer.
Hello, Hello, Hello David!
It's so good to seeyer.
Good morning, Good Morning, Good Morning Lanlan!
It's so good to meetyer!
Good-bye, Good-bye, Tomorrow seeyer!

9

问候歌 (wèn hòu gē)
The Greeting Song

兰兰 (Lánlan) is a girl, 大伟 (Dàwěi) is a boy,

林老师 (Lín lǎoshī / Ms Lin) is their teacher。

他们 (tā men / they) 见面 (jiàn miàn / meet) 说 (shuō / say) 什么 (shén me / what)?

"同学们好!" (tóng xué men hǎo / hello Students) "老师好!" (lǎo shī hǎo / hello teacher)

人人 (rén rén / every person) 都 (dōu / all) 要 (yào / should) 讲 (jiǎng / speak) 礼貌 (lǐ mào / politeness)。

The Greeting Song
By Dr. X. Zhou & T. Gourdon

Lanlan is a girl, David is a boy,
They both like the same toy,
A scooter they both enjoy.
Ms Lin is their teacher,
Language is her main feature.
What do they say when they meet her?
"Hello, students! Hello, Teacher!"
Ms Lin is an excitable creature,
So we all show polite manner to please her.

10 我 你 他
I You and He

我 是 I， 你 是 you，
(I am) (you are)

他 是 he， 她 是 she。
(he is) (she is)

我 们， 你 们 和 他 们
(we) (you) (and) (they)

加 在 一 起 三 扇 门[1]。
(add) (be together) (three doors)

I You and He

By Dr. X. Zhou & T. Gourdon

"wǒ" is "I", "nǐ" is "you",
"tā" is "he", "tā" is "she".
"you" "they" and "we",
What could their meaning be?
There are three doors in them,
As you all can see.

[1] 注:"门"与"们"谐音。

上课
The Lesson Song

wǒ	men	kāi	shǐ	shàng	kè
我	们	开	始	上	课，
we		begin		start lesson	

dà	jiā	zhù	yì	tīng	jiǎng
大	家	注	意	听	讲。
every one		pay attention		listen to teacher's instruction	

tí	wèn	qǐng	xiān	jǔ	shǒu
提	问	请	先	举	手，
ask questions		please	first	raise	hand

bú	yào	suí	biàn	shuō	huà
不	要	随	便	说	话。
shouldn't		casual		talk	

The Lesson Song

By Dr. X. Zhou & T. Gourdon

We start our lesson now,
The teacher will show you how.
Pay attention to the teacher's instruction,
This will be a grand induction.
Raise your hand before making a submission,
Do not talk without permission.

The Number Song

By Dr. X. Zhou & T. Gourdon

One two three four five,
I like to dance the JIVE[1].
Six seven eight nine ten,
He likes to run now and then.
One two three four five six seven,
We all like playing chess,
And feel as though we are in heaven.
Seven six five four three two one
We all like to fly aeroplanes for fun.

[1] Note: JIVE: the name of a type of dance.

A Tongue Twister

sān shì sān, shān shì shān;
三 是 三， 山 是 山；
three is three mountain is mountain

sì shì sì, shí shì shí。
四 是 四， 十 是 十。
four is four ten is ten

bú yào bǎ shān niàn chéng sān,
不 要 把 山 念 成 三，
Don't Prep. mountain read as three

bú yào bǎ shí niàn chéng sì。
不 要 把 十 念 成 四。
Don't Prep. ten read as four

A Tongue Twister

By Dr. X. Zhou & T. Gourdon

"sān" is "three", "shān" is "mountain",
"sì" is "four", "shí" is "ten".
Do not say "shān" as "sān",
Do not say "shí" as "sì".
So as you can see,
"sān、shān、sì、shí",
Are as similar as can be.

pāi shǒu gē
拍 手 歌
The Hand-Clapping Song

nǐ	pāi	yī	wǒ	pāi	yī	yí	ge	xiǎo	háir	chuān	xīn	yī
你	拍	一，	我	拍	一，	一	个	小	孩儿	穿	新	衣。
you	clap	one	I	clap	one			one little child		wear new clothes		

nǐ	pāi	èr	wǒ	pāi	èr	liǎng	ge	xiǎo	háir	chàng	ér	gē
你	拍	二，	我	拍	二，	两	个	小	孩儿	唱	儿	歌。
you	clap	two	I	clap	two			two little children		sing kid song		

nǐ	pāi	sān	wǒ	pāi	sān	sān	ge	xiǎo	háir	pá	dà	shān
你	拍	三，	我	拍	三，	三	个	小	孩儿	爬	大	山。
you	clap	three	I	clap	three			three little children		climb big mountain		

nǐ	pāi	sì	wǒ	pāi	sì	sì	ge	xiǎo	háir	xiě	dà	zì
你	拍	四，	我	拍	四，	四	个	小	孩儿	写	大	字。
you	clap	four	I	clap	four			four little children		write big character		

nǐ	pāi	wǔ	wǒ	pāi	wǔ	wǔ	ge	xiǎo	háir	xué	tiào	wǔ
你	拍	五，	我	拍	五，	五	个	小	孩儿	学	跳	舞。
you	clap	five	I	clap	five			five little children		learn dance		

nǐ	pāi	liù	wǒ	pāi	liù	liù	ge	xiǎo	háir	dǎ	lán	qiú
你	拍	六，	我	拍	六，	六	个	小	孩儿	打	篮	球。
you	clap	six	I	clap	six			six little children		play basketball		

nǐ	pāi	qī	wǒ	pāi	qī	qī	ge	xiǎo	háir	chàng	jīng	xì
你	拍	七，	我	拍	七，	七	个	小	孩儿	唱	京	戏。
you	clap	seven	I	clap	seven			seven little children		sing Peking Opera		

nǐ	pāi	bā	wǒ	pāi	bā	bā	ge	xiǎo	háir	chuī	lǎ	bā
你	拍	八，	我	拍	八，	八	个	小	孩儿	吹	喇	叭。
you	clap	eight	I	clap	eight			eight little children		play trumpet		

nǐ	pāi	jiǔ	wǒ	pāi	jiǔ	jiǔ	ge	xiǎo	háir	tī	zú	qiú
你	拍	九，	我	拍	九，	九	个	小	孩儿	踢	足	球。
you	clap	nine	I	clap	nine			nine little children		play football		

nǐ	pāi	shí	wǒ	pāi	shí	shí	ge	xiǎo	háir	wā	bǎo	shí
你	拍	十，	我	拍	十，	十	个	小	孩儿	挖	宝	石。
you	clap	ten	I	clap	ten			ten little children		dig precious stone		

The Hand-Clapping Song

By Dr. X. Zhou & T. Gourdon

You clap one, I clap one,
One little child wears new clothes for fun;
You clap two, I clap two,
Two little children sing a rhyme to you;
You clap three, I clap three,
Three little children climb a mountain with glee;
You clap four, I clap four,
Four little children write characters on the floor;
You clap five, I clap five,
Five little children learn to dance the JIVE;
You clap six, I clap six,
Six little children play basketball for kicks;
You clap seven, I clap seven,
Seven children sing the Peking Opera in heaven;
You clap eight, I clap eight,
Eight children play trumpet at the gate;
You clap nine, I clap nine,
Nine children play soccer and feel fine;
You clap ten, I clap ten,
Ten children dig for gems.
Will they find them? I don't know when.

15 nǐ shì shéi 你 是 谁?
Who are You?

nǐ	shì	shéi		wǒ	shì	lǐ	xiǎo	méi
你	是	谁?		我	是	李	小	梅。
you	are	who		I	am		Li Xiaomei	

tā	shì	shéi		tā	shì	bái	dà	wěi
他	是	谁?		他	是	白	大	伟;
he	is	who		he	is		Bai Dawei	

hái	yǒu	mǎ	kè	hé	mǎ	lì
还	有	马	克	和	玛	丽,
in addition		Mark		and		Mary

wǒ	men	měi	tiān	zài	yì	qǐ
我	们	每	天	在	一	起。
we		every	day		be together	

Who are You?
By Dr. X. Zhou & T. Gourdon

Who are you?
I am Xiaomei Li,
I am quite friendly;
Who is he?
He is David White,
He's been working all night.
There are also Mark and Mary,
And we all play together near the dairy.

16

shéi a
谁 啊?
Who is It?

A: shéi a / 谁 啊? (who Ah!)   B: wǒ a / 我 啊! (me Ah!)

A: nǐ shì shéi / 你 是 谁? (you are who)   B: wǒ shì lán / 我 是 兰。 (I am Lan)

A: a, lán lan, nǐ hǎo! huān yíng, / 啊, 兰 兰, 你 好! 欢 迎, (Ah! Lanlan hello welcome)

huān yíng, kuài qǐng jìn! / 欢 迎, 快 请 进! (welcome quickly please come in)

A: a, nǐ hǎo ma? / 啊, 你 好 吗? (Ah! you good inter.)   B: a, nǐ hǎo ma? / 啊, 你 好 吗? (Ah! you good inter.)

A&B: a, dà jiā dōu hǎo, hā, hā, / 啊, 大 家 都 好, 哈, 哈, (Ah! we all good, ha, ha,)

hā, hā, hā, hā, hā / 哈, 哈, 哈, 哈, 哈 (ha ha ha ha ha)

1 2 3 4 5 3 1
do re mi fa so mi do!

Who is It?

By Dr. X. Zhou & T. Gourdon

A: Who is it?
B: It's me.
And I am free as a cool morning breeze;
A: Who are you?
B: I am Lanlan from the mainland;
A: Hey, Lanlan, Hello! Welcome, welcome! Please come in,
And let me see your pretty white teeth when you grin;
A: Hey, how are you?
B: Hey, how are you?
A & B: Hey, we are both fine
in the bright sunshine,
ha, ha, ha, ha,ha, ha, ha ……
do re mi fa so mi do!

你 几 岁?
How Old are You?

你今年几岁? 我今年九岁。
you / this year / how old / I / this year / nine years old

他今年几岁? 他今年十岁。
he / this year / how old / he / this year / ten years old

兰兰今年十一岁,
Lanlan / this year / eleven years old

大伟今年十二岁,
David / this year / twelve years old

我们每年大一岁。
we / every year / grow / one year old

How Old are You?
By Dr. X. Zhou & T. Gourdon

How old are you this year?
I am nine this year, Mother dear;
How old is he this year?
He is ten this year, Father dear;
Lanlan is eleven this year, Sister dear;
David is twelve this year, Brother dear;
We are one year older every year,
As long as we live, my dear.

wén jù gē
文具歌
The Stationery Song

chǐ　　　　　　　　　bǐ
尺　is a ruler，笔　is a pen；
ruler　　　　　　　　pen

shū　　　　　　　　　bāo
书　is a book，包　is a bag；
book　　　　　　　　bag

　　　　jiào jiǎn dāo　　　　　jiào xiàng pí
Scissors 叫 剪 刀，eraser 叫 橡 皮，
　　　　call　scissor　　　　　call　eraser

tā men dōu zài shū bāo li
它 们 都 在 书 包 里，
they　all　　in the school bag

měi tiān hé wǒ zài yì qǐ
每 天 和 我 在 一 起。
every day　with　me　　be together

The Stationery Song

By Dr. X. Zhou & T. Gourdon

"chǐ" is a ruler, "bǐ" is a pen;
"shū" is a book, "bāo" is a bag;
These are easy words to repeat again.
If you can the next two retain:
jiǎndāo: scissors and erasers: xiàngpí,
You are certainly doing better than me.
They are all in my school bag,
Keeping me company and for all to see.

19 wǒ de xué xí yòng pǐn
我的学习用品
My Stationery

yī èr sān, sān èr yī, zhè shì wǒ de shū hé bǐ
一二三，三二一，这是我的书和笔；
one two three, three two one, these are my book and pen

yī èr sān sì wǔ liù qī, nà shì jiǎn dāo hé xiàng pí
一二三四五六七，那是剪刀和橡皮。
one two three four five six seven, those are scissor and eraser

yī èr sān, sān èr yī, hái yǒu shū bāo hé máo bǐ
一二三，三二一，还有书包和毛笔。
one two three, three two one, still have school bag and brush pen

My Stationery

By Dr. X. Zhou & T. Gourdon

One two three, three two one,
Now I'm not so glum;
These are my book and pen,
I'm glad I found them again.
One two three four five six seven,
I thought they must have gone to heaven.
Those scissors and that eraser
Were covering them.
One two three, three two one,
Now they are all safely in my school bag
with a brush pen.

20 教室歌 (jiào shì gē)
Classroom Objects

剪刀，橡皮，剪刀，橡皮，
jiǎn dāo / xiàng pí / jiǎn dāo / xiàng pí
scissors / eraser / scissors / eraser

书和笔，书和笔；
shū hé bǐ, shū hé bǐ
book and pen, book and pen

铅笔，钢笔，圆珠笔，
qiān bǐ / gāng bǐ / yuán zhū bǐ
pencil / pen / ball-point pen

毛笔，彩笔和粉笔；
máo bǐ / cǎi bǐ hé fěn bǐ
brush pen / colour pen and powder pen/chalk

桌子，椅子和凳子，
zhuō zi / yǐ zi hé dèng zi
table / chair and stool

还有门窗和教室。
hái yǒu mén chuāng hé jiào shì
in addition door window and classroom

Classroom Objects

By Dr. X. Zhou & T. Gourdon

Scissors, eraser, scissors, eraser,

Snip snip, rub rub, snip snip, rub rub;

Books and pens, books and pens,

Read read, write write, read read, write write

On and on right through the night;

Pencils, ink pens and biros,

Scraping on until the sun peeps

Through the skylight;

Brush pens, texters and chalk,

Desks, chairs and stools,

Waiting silently through the night

For the doors and windows of the classroom

To open and let in the morning light.

21. 这是谁的书?
Whose Book is This?

A: 这 是 谁 的 书?
    this is whose book

B: 这 是 我 的 书。
    this is my book

A: 那 是 谁 的 笔?
    that is whose pen

B: 那 是 你 的 笔。
    that is your pen

A: 我 的 书 包 你 的 尺,
    my school bag your ruler

借 用 一 下 行 不 行?
borrow to use once ok or not

谢 谢! 谢 谢!
thank you thank you

B: 不 客 气!
    not at all

Whose Book is This?

By Dr. X. Zhou & T. Gourdon

Dr. Zhou, where is my book and pen?
Have you taken them again?
Whose book is this?
This is my book I think.
Look, here is my name written in ink.
That is your book and no mistake,
Your perfection, Dr. Zhou, is hard to take.
My school bag and your ruler,
Can I borrow your ruler or not?
Yes, you can borrow it,
But be careful!
It's the only one I've got.
Thanks, thanks a lot!
Not at all, not at all!

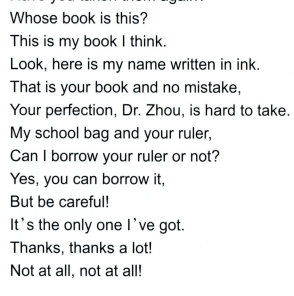

22. 你们知道不知道?
Do You Know or Not?

zhè	shì	shéi	de	shū	bāo	nà	shì	shéi	de	jiǎn	dāo
这	是	谁	的	书	包?	那	是	谁	的	剪	刀?
this	is	whose		school	bag	that	is	whose			scissor

nǐ	men	zhī	dao	bu	zhī	dao
你	们	知	道	不	知	道?
you		know		or	not	

zhè	shì	lán	lan	de	shū	bāo	nà	shì	dà	wěi	de	jiǎn	dāo
这	是	兰	兰	的	书	包,	那	是	大	伟	的	剪	刀,
this	is	Lanlan's			school bag		that	is	David's			scissor	

wǒ	men	dà	jiā	dōu	zhī	dao
我	们	大	家	都	知	道。
we		every one		all	know	

Do You Know or Not?

By Dr. X. Zhou & T. Gourdon

Whose school bag is this?
Does it belong to you, Miss?
And whose scissors are they?
We don't need them today.
Do you know or not?
This is Lanlan's school bag.
Those are David's scissors
wrapped in a rag.
We all know the answer,
No need to nag!

23 yóu xì gē 游戏歌
Let's Play the Game

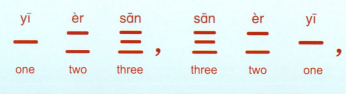

yī èr sān, sān èr yī,
一 二 三， 三 二 一，
one two three three two one

jiǎn dāo shí tou bù
剪 刀， 石 头， 布；
scissors rock cloth

yī èr sān sì wǔ liù qī
一 二 三 四 五 六 七，
one two three four five six seven

wǒ men yì qǐ wánr yóu xì
我 们 一 起 玩儿 游 戏。
we together play game

Let's Play the Game

By Dr. X. Zhou & T. Gourdon

One two three, three two one,
This game is great fun.
Scissors, rock and paper.
One two three four five six seven,
What a funny caper!
Let's play the game together.

28

24 家人歌 (jiā rén gē)
The Family Song

Dad is 爸爸 (bà ba), Mum is 妈妈 (mā ma);

Elder brother 是哥哥 (shì gē ge), younger brother 是弟弟 (shì dì di);

Elder sister 是姐姐 (shì jiě jie), younger sister 是妹妹 (shì mèi mei);

爸爸 妈妈 是 BOSS (bà ba mā ma shì),

我 们 都 是 好 孩 子。 (wǒ men dōu shì hǎo hái zi)

The Family Song

By Dr. X. Zhou & T. Gourdon

Dad is Papa, Mum is Mama;
Elder brother is eldest, Younger brother is youngest;
One to the other can be the best,
Or perhaps just a pest!
Elder sister is eldest, Younger sister is youngest;
To each other they are always the best
And never just a pest!
Papa and Mama are the family BOSS,
We children are good at staying out of trouble,
So we don't make them cross.

25. 我爱爸爸和妈妈
wǒ ài bà ba hé mā ma

I Love Dad and Mum

wǒ jiā yǒu qī ge rén
我 家 有 七 个 人。
My family　　have　　seven people

wǒ yǒu bà ba hé mā ma
我 有 爸 爸 和 妈 妈。
I　have　　Dad　　and　　Mum

wǒ yǒu gē ge hé jiě jie
我 有 哥 哥 和 姐 姐,
I　have　elder brother　and　elder sister

yě yǒu dì di hé mèi mei
也 有 弟 弟 和 妹 妹。
also have　younger brother　and　younger sister

wǒ ài bà ba hé mā ma
我 爱 爸 爸 和 妈 妈。
I　love　　Dad　　and　　Mum

wǒ ài gē ge hé jiě jie
我 爱 哥 哥 和 姐 姐,
I　love　elder brother　and　elder sister

yě ài dì di hé mèi mei
也 爱 弟 弟 和 妹 妹。
also　love　younger brother　and　younger sister

I Love Dad and Mum

By Dr. X. Zhou & T. Gourdon

My family of seven,
Are so happy and feel like
We are in heaven.
I have Dad and Mum,
An elder brother and sister,
In Chinese this can be a tongue twister;
I also have a younger sister and brother,
That's enough, no need for any other;
I love Mum and Dad,
Big sister and brother, by gad!
And little brother and sister
Make me wonderfully glad,
So we are never sad!

中文词汇表

(简繁对照)

No. 1 字母歌 The Chinese Alphabet Song

1. 字母 【zìmǔ】 名 alphabet
2. 歌 【gē】 名 song
3. 这(這) 【zhè】 代 this
4. 是 【shì】 动 is/am/are
5. 汉语(漢語) 【Hànyǔ】 名 Chinese
6. 人 【rén】 名 human being; person
7. 会(會) 【huì】 动 can; be able to
8. 唱 【chàng】 动 sing
9. 乐(樂) 【lè】 形 happy

No. 2 笔画歌 The Character Stroke Song

1. 笔画(筆畫) 【bǐhuà】 名 stroke
2. 点(點) 【diǎn】 名 dot
3. 横 【héng】 名 horizontal stroke
4. 竖(豎) 【shù】 名 vertical stroke
5. 撇 【piě】 名 left-falling stroke
6. 捺 【nà】 名 right-falling stroke
7. 还有(還有) 【háiyǒu】 副 also; too
8. 提 【tí】 名 rising stroke
9. 和 【hé】 连 and
10. 勾(句) 【gōu】 名 hook
11. 写(寫) 【xiě】 动 write
12. 字 【zì】 名 word; character
13. 数(數) 【shǔ】 动 count
14. 永远(永遠) 【yǒngyuǎn】 副 forever
15. 记(記) 【jì】 动 remember
16. 心头(心頭) 【xīntóu】 名 heart; mind

No. 3 四声歌 The Four Tones Song

1. 妈(媽) 【mā】 名 Mum
2. 麻 【má】 名/形/动 flax; numb; tingle
3. 马(馬) 【mǎ】 名 horse
4. 骂(罵) 【mà】 动 scold; swear
5. 第 【dì】 前缀 sequential marker
6. 一 【yī】 数 one
7. 二 【èr】 数 two
8. 三 【sān】 数 three
9. 四 【sì】 数 four
10. 声调(聲調) 【shēngdiào】 名 tone
11. 忘 【wàng】 动 forget
12. 不 【bù】 副 not; no
13. 忘不了 【wàngbùliǎo】 can't forget

No. 4 山水歌 Mountains and Water

1. 山 【shān】 名 mountain
2. 水 【shuǐ】 名 water
3. 日 【rì】 名 the sun
4. 月 【yuè】 名 the moon
5. 我 【wǒ】 代 I
6. 爱(愛) 【ài】 动 love
7. 多么(多麼) 【duōme】 副 so
8. 美 【měi】 形 pretty

No. 5 林火歌 Forests and Fire

1. 林 【lín】 名 forest
2. 火 【huǒ】 名 fire
3. 木 【mù】 名 tree
4. 上 【shàng】 名 on; above
5. 成 【chéng】 动 become

6. 着火(著火)	【zháohuǒ】动	catch fire	
7. 来(來)	【lái】动	come	
8. 救	【jiù】动	rescue	
9. 用	【yòng】动	use	
10. 泼(潑)	【pō】动	pour	
11. 开(開)	【kāi】动	open	
12. 口	【kǒu】名	mouth	
13. 笑	【xiào】动	laugh	
14. 呵呵	【hēhē】叹	the sound of laughter	

11. 看	【kàn】动	see; look	
12. 完	【wán】动	finish	

No. 8 你好！Hello!

1. 你	【nǐ】代	you	
2. 老师(老師)	【lǎoshī】名	teacher	
3. 大伟(大偉)	【Dàwěi】名	David (name)	
4. 早	【zǎo】名	morning	
5. 你早	【nǐ zǎo】	Good morning	
6. 兰兰(蘭蘭)	【Lánlan】名	name	
7. 再见(再見)	【zàijiàn】动	Good-bye	
8. 明天	【míngtiān】名	tomorrow	

No. 6 人口歌 The Population Song

1. 人口	【rénkǒu】名	population	
2. 中国(中國)	【Zhōngguó】名	China	
3. 十	【shí】数	ten	
4. 亿(億)	【yì】量	a hundred million	
5. 站	【zhàn】动	stand	
6. 在	【zài】动/介	be; at	
7. 一起	【yìqǐ】副	together	
8. 数(數)	【shǔ】动	count	
9. 清	【qīng】形	clear	
10. 全	【quán】形	whole	
11. 世界	【shìjiè】名	world	

No. 9 问候歌 The Greeting Song

1. 问候(問候)	【wènhòu】动	greet	
2. 女孩儿	【nǚháir】名	girl	
3. 男孩儿	【nánháir】名	boy	
4. 他	【tā】代	he	
5. 们(們)	【mén】后缀	plural marker	
6. 他们(他們)	【tāmen】代	they	
7. 见面(見面)	【jiànmiàn】动	meet	
8. 说(説)	【shuō】动	say	
9. 什么(甚麼)	【shénme】代	what	
10. 同学(同學)	【tóngxué】名	student; classmate	
11. 都	【dōu】副	all	
12. 要	【yào】动	must; should	
13. 讲(講)	【jiǎng】动	speak	
14. 礼貌(禮貌)	【lǐmào】名	politeness	

No. 7 大好河山 Grand Rivers and Mountains

1. 大	【dà】形	big	
2. 好	【hǎo】形	good	
3. 长江(長江)	【Cháng Jiāng】名	the Yangtze River	
4. 黄河	【Huáng Hé】名	the Yellow River	
5. 大运河(大運河)	【Dàyùn Hé】名	the Grand Canal	
6. 黄山	【Huáng Shān】名	Mount Huangshan	
7. 泰山	【Tài Shān】名	Mount Taishan	
8. 庐山(廬山)	【Lú Shān】名	Mount Lushan	
9. 西湖	【Xī Hú】名	the West Lake	
10. 洞庭湖	【Dòngtíng Hú】名	the Dongting Lake	

No. 10 我你他 I You and He

1. 她	【tā】代	she	
2. 我们(我們)	【wǒmen】代	we	
3. 你们(你們)	【nǐmen】代	you	
4. 加	【jiā】动	add; plus	
5. 扇	【shàn】量	measure word for door	
6. 门(門)	【mén】名	door	

No. 11 上课 The Lesson Song

1. 上课(上課) 【shàngkè】动 start class
2. 开始(開始) 【kāishǐ】动 begin; start
3. 大家 【dàjiā】名 all; everybody
4. 注意 【zhùyì】动 pay attention to
5. 听讲(聽講) 【tīngjiǎng】动 listen to teacher's instrnction
6. 提问(提問) 【tíwèn】动 ask questions
7. 请(請) 【qǐng】动 please
8. 先 【xiān】副 first
9. 举手(舉手) 【jǔshǒu】动 raise hand
10. 随便(隨便) 【suíbiàn】副 casual
11. 说话(説話) 【shuōhuà】动 talk

No. 12 数字歌 The Number Song

1. 数字(數字) 【shùzì】名 number
2. 五 【wǔ】数 five
3. 喜欢(喜歡) 【xǐhuan】动 like
4. 跳舞 【tiàowǔ】动 dance
5. 六 【liù】数 six.
6. 七 【qī】数 seven
7. 八 【bā】数 eight.
8. 九 【jiǔ】数 nine
9. 跑步 【pǎobù】动 run
10. 下棋 【xiàqí】动 play chess
11. 飞机(飛機) 【fēijī】名 aeroplane

No. 13 顺口溜 A Tongue Twister

1. 顺口溜(順口溜)【shùnkǒuliū】名 tongue twister
2. 把 【bǎ】介
3. 念(唸) 【niàn】动 read aloud

No. 14 拍手歌 The Hand–Clapping Song

1. 拍 【pāi】动 clap; pat
2. 个 【gè】量 measure word for people
3. 小孩儿 【xiǎohái r】 little child
4. 穿 【chuān】动 wear
5. 新衣 【xīnyī】名 new clothes
6. 两 【liǎng】数 two
7. 打 【dǎ】动 play
8. 篮球 【lánqiú】名 basketball
9. 京戏(京戲) 【jīngxì】名 Peking Opera
10. 吹 【chuī】动 blow
11. 喇叭 【lǎba】名 trumpet
12. 踢 【tī】动 kick
13. 足球 【zúqiú】名 football; soccer
14. 挖 【wā】动 dig
15. 宝石(寶石) 【bǎoshí】名 gem; precious stone

No. 15 你是谁？Who are You?

1. 谁(誰) 【shéi】代 who
2. 李 【Lǐ】名 plum (a surname)
3. 小梅 【Xiǎoméi】名 little plum (name)
4. 马克(馬克) 【Mǎkè】名 Mark (name)
5. 玛丽(瑪麗) 【Mǎlì】名 Mary (name)
6. 每 【měi】代 every; each

No. 16 谁啊？Who is It?

1. 啊 【ā】叹 ah, oh
2. 欢迎(歡迎) 【huānyíng】动 welcome
3. 快 【kuài】副 fast; quick
4. 进(進) 【jìn】动 enter; come in

No. 17 你几岁？How Old are You?

1. 几(幾) 【jǐ】数 how many
2. 岁(歲) 【suì】名 year (of age)
3. 今年 【jīnnián】名 this (year)

No. 18 文具歌 The Stationery Song

1. 文具 【wénjù】名 stationery
2. 尺 【chǐ】名 ruler
3. 笔(筆) 【bǐ】名 pen

4. 书包（書包）	【shūbāo】名	schoolbag
5. 叫	【jiào】动	call
6. 剪刀	【jiǎndāo】名	scissors
7. 橡皮	【xiàngpí】名	rubber; eraser
8. 它	【tā】代	it
9. 它们（它們）	【tāmen】代	they
10. 里（裏）	【lǐ】名	in

No. 19　我的学习用品 My Stationery

1. 学习（學習）	【xuéxí】动	study; learn
2. 用品	【yòngpǐn】名	supplies
3. 那	【nà】代	that
4. 毛笔（毛筆）	【máobǐ】名	brush pen

No. 20　教室歌 Classroom Objects

1. 教室	【jiàoshì】名	classroom
2. 用具	【yòngjù】名	utensil
3. 铅笔（鉛筆）	【qiānbǐ】名	pencil
4. 钢笔（鋼筆）	【gāngbǐ】名	pen
5. 圆珠笔（圓珠筆）	【yuánzhūbǐ】名	ball-point pen
6. 彩笔（彩筆）	【cǎibǐ】名	colour pencil or pen
7. 粉笔（粉筆）	【fěnbǐ】名	chalk
8. 桌子	【zhuōzi】名	table; desk
9. 凳子	【dèngzi】名	stool
10. 窗	【chuāng】名	window
11. 椅子	【yǐzi】名	chair

No. 21　这是谁的书？Whose Book is This?

1. 谁的（誰的）	【shéide】	whose
2. 借	【jiè】动	borrow
3. 一下	【yíxià】数量	one time; a short while
4. 行	【xíng】动	O.K.
5. 谢谢（謝謝）	【xièxie】动	thank
6. 客气	【kèqi】形	courteous

No. 22　你们知道不知道？Do You Know or Not?

1. 知道	【zhīdao】动	know

No. 23　游戏歌 Let's Play The Game!

1. 游戏（遊戲）	【yóuxì】名	game
2. 石头（石頭）	【shítou】名	stone; rock
3. 布	【bù】名	cloth
4. 玩	【wán】动	play

No. 24　家人歌 The Family Song

1. 爸爸	【bàba】名	dad
2. 妈妈(媽媽)	【māma】名	mum
3. 哥哥	【gēge】名	elder brother
4. 弟弟	【dìdi】名	younger brother
5. 姐姐	【jiějie】名	elder sister
6. 妹妹	【mèimei】名	younger sister

No. 25　我爱爸爸和妈妈 I Love Mum and Dad

1. 也	【yě】副	also; too

英文词汇表

(简繁对照)

No.1　The Chinese Alphabet Song

1. the	Art.	定冠词(定冠詞)
2. Chinese	N.	汉语(漢語)
3. alphabet	N.	字母
4. song	N.	歌,歌曲
5. this	Pron.	这(這)
6. we	Pron.	我们(我們)
7. are	V.	是
8. all	N.	全部
9. happy	A.	高兴,愉快,幸福(高興,愉快,幸福)
10. when	Conj.	当……的时候(當……的時候)
11. sing	V.	唱
12. along	Adv.	一起

No.2　The Character Stroke Song

1. character	N.	汉字(漢字)
2. stroke	N.	笔画(筆畫)
3. a	Art.	不定冠词(不定冠詞)
4. dot	N.	点(點)
5. line	N.	横
6. horizontal	A.	水平的
7. vertical	A.	垂直的
8. slant	V.	倾斜(傾斜)
9. left	A.	左边(左邊)
10. right	A.	右边(右邊)
11. tick	N.	记号,提(記號,提)
12. hook	N.	勾(句)
13. mark	N.	标记(標記)
14. in	Prep.	在……里面(在……裏面)
15. your	Pron.	你的,你们的(你的,你們的)
16. book	N.	书(書)
17. then	Adv.	接着(接著)
18. count	V.	数(數)
19. basic	A.	基本的
20. write	V.	写(寫)

21. forever	Adv.	永远(永遠)
22. should	Aux.	应该(應該)
23. remember	V.	记住(記住)

No.3　The Four Tones Song

1. rhyme	N.	儿歌(兒歌)
2. four	Num.	四
3. tone	N.	声调(聲調)
4. Mum	N.	妈妈(媽媽)
5. illustrate	V.	说明(説明)
6. number	N.	数字(數字)
7. one	Num.	一
8. mean	V.	意思是……
9. numb	A./V.	麻木/使麻木
10. represent	V.	表示
11. two	Num.	二
12. horse	N.	马(馬)
13. three	Num.	三
14. of course		当然(當然)
15. scold	V.	骂,责备(罵,責備)
16. fourth	Num.	第四
17. such as		例如
18. told	V.	告诉(告訴)
19. not	Adv.	不,没
20. so	Adv.	如此,那么(如此,那麼)
21. bold	A.	无畏的
22. just	Adv.	就,正好
23. like	Prep.	像……一样(像……一樣)
24. music	N.	音乐(音樂)
25. note	N.	音符
26. must	Aux.	必须(必須)
27. learn	V.	学(學)
28. by rote		熟记(熟記)

No.4　Mountains and Rivers

1. mountain	N.	山

2. water	N.	水	
3. sun	N.	太阳(太陽)	
4. moon	N.	月亮	
5. love	V.	喜爱(喜愛)	
6. climb	V.	爬(山)	
7. excitement	N.	激动(激動)	
8. and	Conj.	和	
9. glee	N.	高兴(高興)	
10. high	A.	高	
11. above	A.	上面	
12. river	N.	河流	
13. pretty	A.	美;可爱(美;可愛)	

No. 5   Forests and Fire

1. forest	N.	森林
2. fire	N.	火
3. spring	V.	跳跃(跳躍)
4. fountain	N.	喷泉(噴泉)
5. tree	N.	树(樹)
6. grow	V.	生长(生長)
7. catch	V.	拿,着火(拿,著火)
8. flame	N.	火焰(火焰)
9. get	V.	得到,变得(得到,變得)
10. people	N.	人们(人們)
11. come	V.	过来(過來)
12. pour	V.	泼水(潑水)
13. douse	V.	扑灭(撲滅)
14. laugh	V.	笑
15. mouth	N.	嘴巴;口
16. open	V.	张开(張開)
17. wide	V.	宽(寬)

No. 6   The Population Song

1. population	N.	人口
2. billion	Num.	十亿(十億)
3. stand	V.	站立
4. together	Adv.	一起
5. amount	N.	数目(數目)
6. impossible	A.	不可能
7. world	N.	世界

No. 7   Grand Rivers and Mountains

1. grand	A.	伟大的,了不起(偉大的,
		了不起)
2. Yangtze River	N.	长江(長江)
3. Yellow River	N.	黄河
4. Grand Canal	N.	大运河(大運河)
5. definitely	Adv.	确定地(確定地)
6. banal	A.	平凡的
7. Yellow Mountains	N.	黄山
8. Tai Mountains	N.	泰山
9. Lu Mountains	N.	庐山(廬山)
10. spectacular	A.	壮观的(壯觀的)
11. summer	N.	夏天
12. rain	N.	雨
13. West Lake	N.	西湖
14. Tai Lake	N.	太湖
15. Dongting Lake	N.	洞庭湖
16. certainly	Adv.	肯定地
17. fake	N.	虚构(虛構)
18. timeless	A.	永恒的
19. breath	N.	呼吸
20. breath-taking		令人惊奇的(令人驚奇的)
21. keep	V.	维持,保持(維持,保持)
22. awake	A.	醒着(醒著)
23. endless	A.	无终止的(無終止的)
24. great	A.	了不起的

No. 8   Hello!

1. Hello	Int.	你好
2. teacher	N.	老师(老師)
3. greet	V.	打招呼
4. greetyer		greet you 的缩写(greet you 的縮寫)
5. see	V.	见,看见(見,看見)
6. seeyer		see you 的缩写(see you 的縮寫)
7. good	A.	好
8. morning	N.	早上
9. good morning		早上好
10. meet	V.	见面(見面)
11. meetyer		meet you 的缩写(meet you 的縮寫)
12. good-bye		再见(再見)
13. tomorrow	N.	明天

No. 9   The Greeting Song

1. Lanlan	N.	兰兰(蘭蘭)

2. David	N.	大伟(大偉)	
3. girl	N.	女孩儿	
4. boy	N	男孩儿	
5. both	Adv.	两者……都(兩者……都)	
6. like	V.	喜欢(喜歡)	
7. same	A.	同样(同樣)	
8. toy	N.	玩具	
9. scooter	N.	小型电单车(小型電單車)	
10. enjoy	V.	喜爱(喜愛)	
11. Ms.	N.	小姐	
12. language	N.	语言(語言)	
13. main	A.	主要的	
14. feature	N.	特征,特点(特徵,特點)	
15. what	Pron.	什么(甚麼)	
16. they	Pron.	他/她们(他/她們)	
17. say	V.	说(說)	
18. student	N.	学生(學生)	
19. excitable	A.	易激动的,易兴奋的(易激動的,易興奮的)	
20. creature	N.	创造物,人(創造物,人)	
21. show	V.	表现,展现(表現,展現)	
22. polite	A.	礼貌的(禮貌的)	
23. manner	N.	举止(舉止)	
24. please	V.	(使)高兴〔(使)高興〕	

No. 10　I You and He

1. I	Pron.	我
2. you	Pron.	你
3. he	Pron.	他
4. she	Pron	她
5. door	N.	门(門)
6. can	Aux.	能,能够

No. 11　The Lesson Song

1. lesson	N.	课(課)
2. start	V.	开始(開始)
3. now	N.	现在(現在)
4. how	Pron.	怎样(怎樣)
5. pay attention to		集中注意力
6. instruction	N.	指令
7. induction	N.	归纳(歸納)
8. raise	V.	举(舉)
9. hand	N.	手

10. before	Prep.	在……之前
11. make	V.	做
12. submission	N.	提交
13. talk	V.	讲话(講話)
14. without	Prep.	没有
15. permission	N.	同意

No. 12　The Number Song

1. four	Num.	四
2. five	Num.	五
3. dance	V.	跳舞
4. six	Num.	六
5. seven	Num.	七
6. eight	Num.	八
7. nine	Num.	九
8. ten	Num.	十
9. run	V.	跑步
10. play	V.	玩
11. chess	N.	棋
12. as though		好像
13. heaven	N.	天堂
14. fly	V.	飞(飛)
15. aeroplane	N.	飞机(飛機)
16. fun	N.	快乐,开心(快樂,開心)

No. 13　A Tongue Twister

1. tongue	N.	舌头(舌頭)
2. twist	V.	曲折
3. tongue twister		绕口令(繞口令)
4. similar	A.	相似的

No. 14　The Hand-Clapping Song

1. clap	V.	拍手
2. little	A.	小的
3. child	N.	孩子
4. new	A.	新的
5. floor	N.	地板
6. basketball	N.	篮球
7. kick	V.	踢
8. Pekin Opera		京戏(京戲)
9. trumpet	N.	喇叭
10. gate	N.	门(門)

11. soccer	N.	足球	
12. dig	V.	挖	
13. gem	N.	宝石(寶石)	
14. find	V.	找到	
15. know	V.	知道	

No. 15　Who are You?

1. who	Pron.	谁(誰)	
2. quite	Adv.	很	
3. friend	N.	朋友	
4. work	V.	工作,干活(工作,幹活)	
5. night	N.	晚上	
6. all night		通宵	
7. there	Adv.	那儿	
8. near	A.	近的	
9. dairy	N.	农场(農場)	

No. 16　Who is It?

1. free	A.	自由的	
2. cool	A.	凉爽(涼爽)	
3. breeze	N.	微风(微風)	
4. mainland	N.	大陆(大陸)	
5. welcome	V.	欢迎(歡迎)	
6. please	V.	请(請)	
7. come in		进来(進來)	
8. let	V.	让(讓)	
9. white	A.	白色	
10. teeth	N.	牙齿(牙齒)	
11. grin	V.	露齿而笑(露齒而笑)	
12. hey	Int.	嗨	
13. fine	A.	好的,安然无恙的	
14. bright	A.	明亮的	
15. sunshine	N.	阳光(陽光)	

No. 17　How Old are You?

1. old	A.	老的	
2. year	N.	年	
3. this year		今年	
4. mother	N.	母亲	
5. dear	A.	亲爱的(親愛的)	
6. father	N.	父亲	
7. sister	N.	姐妹	

8. brother	N.	兄弟	
9. every	A.	每一	
10. every year		每一年	
11. live	V.	活着(活著)	

No. 18　The Stationery Song

1. stationery	N.	文具	
2. ruler	N.	尺	
3. pen	N.	笔(筆)	
4. book	N.	书(書)	
5. bag	N.	包	
6. easy	A.	容易的	
7. repeat	A.	重复的(重復的)	
8. again	Adv.	又一次	
9. next	Adv.	下一个	
10. retain	V.	记住(記住)	
11. scissors	N.	剪刀	
12. eraser	N.	橡皮	
13. better	A.	更好的	
14. School bag	N.	书包(書包)	
15. company	N.	做伴	

No. 19　My stationery

1. glum	A.	闷闷不乐(悶悶不樂)	
2. glad	A.	高兴(高興)	
3. found	V.	找到	
4. thought	V.	想	
5. go	V.	去	
6. cover	V.	覆盖(覆蓋)	
7. safely	Adv.	安全地	
8. brush pen		毛笔(毛筆)	

No. 20　Classroom Objects

1. classroom	N.	教室	
2. object	N.	物品	
3. snip	V.	剪	
4. rub	V.	(用橡皮)擦	
5. read	V.	读(讀)	
6. right	Adv.	正好,就这样(正好,就這樣)	
7. on	Adv.	连续地(連續地)	
8. write	v.	写(寫)	

9. through	Prep.	(指时间)从头到尾〔(指時間)從頭到尾〕	
10. pencil	N.	铅笔(鉛筆)	
11. ink	N.	墨水	
12. ink pen		钢笔(鋼筆)	
13. biro	N.	圆珠笔(圓珠筆)	
14. scrape	V.	削	
15. until	Prep.	直到	
16. peep	V.	偷看	
17. skylight	N.	天窗	
18. texter	N.	墨水笔(墨水筆)	
19. chalk	N.	粉笔(粉筆)	
20. desk	N.	书桌,写字台(書桌,寫字檯)	
21. chair	N.	椅子	
22. stool	N.	凳子	
23. wait	V.	等,等候	
24. silently	Adv.	安静地	
25. window	N.	窗	
26. light	N.	光	

No. 21   Whose Book is This?

1. whose	Pron.	谁的(誰的)
2. where	Pron.	哪里(哪裏)
3. take	V.	拿
4. mistake	N.	错误(錯誤)
5. perfection	N.	完美
6. hard	A.	难(難)
7. borrow	V.	借
8. careful	A.	小心的
9. thank	V.	谢谢(謝謝)
10. thanks a lot		多谢(多謝)
11. not at all		不客气(不客氣)

No. 22   Do You Know or Not?

1. belong to		属于(屬於)
2. need	V.	需要
3. today	N.	今天
4. answer	N.	答案
5. nag	V.	唠叨

No. 23   Let's Play the Game!

1. game	N.	游戏(遊戲)
2. rock	N.	石头(石頭)
3. paper	N.	纸(紙)
4. funny	A.	有趣的
5. caper	N.	嬉戏(嬉戲)

No. 24   The Family Song

1. family	N.	家
2. Dad	N.	爸爸
3. Mum	N.	妈妈(媽媽)
4. elder brother		哥哥
5. eldest	A.	最老的
6. younger brother		弟弟
7. youngest	A.	最小的
8. best	A.	最好的
9. perhaps	Adv.	也许(也許)
10. pest	N.	害虫(害蟲)
11. elder sister		姐姐
12. younger sister		妹妹
13. each	Pron.	每个
14. each other		互相
15. never	Adv.	从不(從不)
16. boss	N.	老板(老闆)
17. good at		擅长于(擅長於)
18. stay	V.	停留
19. trouble	N.	麻烦(麻煩)
20. out of trouble		避免麻烦(避免麻煩)
21. make	V.	使得
22. cross	A.	生气的(生氣的)

No. 25   I Love Mum and Dad

1. feel like	V.	感觉(感覺)
2. enough	A.	足够的
3. wonderfully	Adv.	精彩的
4. sad	A.	伤心的,悲哀的,忧郁的(傷心的,悲哀的,憂鬱的)

《晓康歌谣学汉语》总目录

第一集

1. 字母歌 (The Chinese Alphabet Song)
2. 笔画歌 (The Character Stroke Song)
3. 四声歌 (The Four Tones Song)
4. 山水歌 (Mountains and Water)
5. 林火歌 (Forests and Fire)
6. 人口歌 (The Population Song)
7. 大好河山 (Grand Rivers and Mountains)
8. 你好！(Hello!)
9. 问候歌 (The Greeting Song)
10. 我你他 (I You and He)
11. 上课 (The Lesson Song)
12. 数字歌 (The Number Song)
13. 顺口溜 (A Tongue Twister)
14. 拍手歌 (The Hand-Clapping Song)
15. 你是谁？(Who Are You?)
16. 谁啊？(Who Is It?)
17. 你几岁？(How Old Are You?)
18. 文具歌 (The Stationery Song)
19. 我的学习用品 (My Stationery)
20. 教室歌 (Classroom Objects)
21. 这是谁的书？(Whose Book Is This?)
22. 你们知道不知道？(Do You Know or Not?)
23. 游戏歌 (Let's Play The Game!)
24. 家人歌 (The Family Song)
25. 我爱爸爸和妈妈 (I Love Dad and Mum)

第二集

26. 职业歌 (The Occupation Song)
27. 宠物歌 (The Pet Song)
28. 小狗小猫真可爱
    (Little Dogs and Cats Are Really Cute)
29. 我的好伙伴 (My Best Mate)
30. 打虎歌 (The Tiger-Hunting Song)
31. 青蛙歌 (The Frog Song)
32. 十二生肖歌 (The Twelve Birth Animals)
33. 动物歌 (Wild Animals)
34. 东方和西方 (East And West)
35. 我会说汉语 (I Can Speak Chinese)
36. 国名歌 (The Country Name Song)
37. 国籍歌 (The Nationality Song)
38. 你是哪国人？(What Country Are You From?)
39. 我和妹妹是澳洲人
    (My Sister and I Are Australian)
40. 运动歌 (The Sports Song)
41. 体育运动 (Sporting Activities)
42. 我们都喜欢运动 (We All Like Sports)
43. 我的脸 (My Face)
44. 我的朋友 (My Friend)
45. 同学加朋友 (Classmates And Friends)
46. 你上几年级？(What Year Are You In?)
47. 真好吃！(Really Yummy!)
48. 西餐歌 (The Western Food Song)
49. 你想吃什么？(What Do You Want To Eat?)
50. 我们爱吃中国菜 (We Love Chinese Food)

第三集

51. 一天又一天 (Day By Day)
52. 天天有收获 (Every Day Achivements)
53. 钟点歌 (The Time Song)
54. 过年真热闹！(The New Year Song)
55. 节日歌 (The Festival Song)
56. 节日吃什么？(The Festival Food Song）
57. 中国茶（Chinese Tea）
58. 生活歌 (Song of Daily Life)
59. 活动歌 (The Activity Song)
60. 你在做什么？(What Are You Doing?)

61. 我喜欢看书 (I Like Reading)
62. 放风筝 (Flying Kites)
63. 排队歌 (Line Up Quickly)
64. 方位歌 (The Position Song)
65. 住房歌 (The Home Song)
66. 你在客厅做什么?
    (What Are You Doing in the Lounge?)
67. 家电歌 (Electric Gadgets)
68. 我的衣服 (My Clothes)
69. 颜色歌 (The Colour Song)
70. 服装歌 (The Fashion Song)
71. 这件衣服怎么样? (How About These Clothes?)
72. 真糟糕! (Really Bad!)
73. 买东西 (The Shopping Song)
74. 水果歌 (The Fruit Song)
75. 多吃水果身体好 (Fruit is Good For You)
76. 水果怎么卖? (How Do You Sell Fruit?)
77. 甜不甜? (Sweet or Not?)
78. 去书店 (Let's Go To The Book Store)
79. 一共多少钱? (How Much Is It Altogether?)
80. 你家住哪里? (Where Does Your Family Live?)
81. 你在哪儿工作? (Where Do You Work?)
82. 称呼歌 (The Kinship Terms Song)
83. 朋友来电话 (A Call From A Friend)
84. 我想请你去吃饭 (Meal Invitation)
85. 今天谁点菜?
    (Who Will Order The Dishes Today?)

第四集

86. 天气预报 (Weather Report)
87. 天气很不好 (Very Bad Weather)
88. 四季歌 (The Four Seasons Song)
89. 北京的天气 (Beijing's Weather)
90. 课程歌 (School Subjects)
91. 你今天上什么课?
    (What Lessons Do You Have Today?)
92. 你家离学校有多远?
    (How Far Is It From Your Home To School?)

93. 你每天怎么去上学?
    (How Do You Go To School Every Day?)
94. 怎么走? (How To Go?)
95. 市中心 (The City Centre Song)
96. 方向歌 (Directions)
97. 交通歌 (The Transport Song)
98. 影片歌 (The Movie Song)
99. 中国艺术 (Chinese Arts)
100. 今晚有演出 (Tonight's Performance)
101. 生日礼物 (Birthday Presents)
102. 比一比 (Let's Compare)
103. 七个好兄弟 (Seven Good Brothers)
104. 真倒霉! (Really Bad Luck!)
105. 旅行用品 (Travel Items)
106. 旅游歌 (Song of Travel)
107. 地名歌 (The Place Names Song)
108. 奥运歌 (The Olympic Games Song)
109. 你假期都在做什么?
     (What Did You Do On Holiday?)
110. 你假期过得怎么样? (How Was Your Holiday)
111. 他这个人怎么样?
     (What Do You Think Of This Person?)
112. 中国人的姓真复杂!
     (Chinese Surnames Are Really Complicated!)
113. 校园活动真丰富!
     (After-school Activities Are Really Exciting!)
114. 你用电脑做什么?
     (What Do You Use A Computer For?)
115. 客气得不得了! (Too Polite!)
116. 你为什么打工? (What Do You Work for?)
117. 你存钱想做什么?
     (What Do You Want To Save For?)
118. 你爸妈最会说你什么?
     (What Do Your Parents Nag About Most?)
119. 拉手歌 (The Hand-holding Song)
120. 祝福歌 (The Song of Good Wishes)

作者简介

周晓康： 1978年考入杭州大学(今浙江大学)外语系，获英国语言文学学士、硕士学位。1985年留校任教，在杭州大学中文系教对外汉语、公共英语、语言学概论等，同时进修中文系现代汉语研究生课程。1987年考入北京大学英语系，攻读英国语言文学博士学位，同时在北京大学中文系进修现代汉语和历史语言学。1989年赴澳，随后就读澳大利亚墨尔本大学语言学系，1993年通过澳大利亚翻译局翻译资格考试，获得澳大利亚翻译局注册三级翻译资格。1994年赴英国威尔士大学卡的夫学院调研汉语系统功能生成计算语言学模式。1998年获墨尔本大学语言学博士学位。发表学术论文五十余篇，其中《论汉语语序的语篇功能》获北京大学"五四"青年学者优秀论文奖一等奖。1999年就读拉筹伯大学(La Trobe University)教育系，获教育学研究生文凭。2000年至今任教于墨尔本半岛学校。在澳大利亚的对外汉语教学中最突出的成就为编写语言教学歌谣近280首。2008年12月获第9届国际汉语教学研讨会创新示范课奖。2009年2月获新金山教育基金2008年全澳优秀中文教师奖。

Dr. Xiaokang Zhou: Graduated in 1980s from Department of Foreign Languages, Hangzhou University (now Zhejiang University), China, with a Bachelor degree and a Master of Arts degree in The English Language and Literature. She was employed by the same university to teach Chinese as a Foreign Language, English, General Linguistics and Modern Linguistics in the Chinese Department, where she also studied the postgraduate course of Modern Chinese. Having passed the entry examinations she was accepted by Peking University as a Ph.D. candidate in the English Department. During her Ph. D. candidature in Peking University, she studied Modern Chinese Grammar and Historical Linguistics in the Department of Chinese. In November 1989, she came to Australia as a visiting scholar and continued her Ph. D. study in the Department of Linguistics, the University of Melbourne, focusing on Western Linguistics and Systemic Functional Grammar, and received her Ph. D. degree in Linguistics from The University of Melbourne in 1998. In 1999 she studied in Department of Education of La Trobe University and received her Graduate Diploma in Education from La Trobe University at the end of the same year. She was employed to teach English as a Second Language as well as Chinese at the Peninsula School in 2000 and has been teaching there since then. Apart from Linguistics and Education, she also holds a qualification as a NAATI (National Authority of Accredited Translators and Interpreters) Level 3 Mandarin-English translator after passing its qualifying examination in 1993. The most significant contribution she made to the Chinese language education in Australia is the series of Dr. Zhou's Rhymes for learning Chinese (about 280 rhymes), In December 2008 she received the International Award for Excellence in Innovative Teaching of Chinese from the Office of Chinese Language Council International and was awarded the Most Excellent Chinese Teacher of 2008 by the Golden Land Education Foundations in February 2009.

编后记

新年伊始,在北京大学出版社汉语及语言学编辑部的精心策划和专业指导下,《晓康歌谣学汉语》(Dr. Zhou's Rhymes for Learning Chinese)终于要以其崭新的面貌和引人入胜的动画卡拉OK形式正式出版了。在此,我要向《晓康歌谣学汉语》北大版创作团队表示最真诚的祝贺和感谢:

责任编辑:旷书文　　　　　演唱、中英文朗诵:Angela Ha
中文朗诵、录音:于永杰　　　动　　画:阿　蓝
伴奏、合成:方　雄、罗　剑　　版式设计:华　伦
英文朗诵:Jude and Will Harper, Angela Ha and Robin Du

没有以上每个成员齐心协力的精诚合作,夜以继日的辛勤耕耘,就不可能有这一部集语言、韵文、音乐、美术、动画、卡拉OK于一体的精品之作的问世。尤其值得一提的是团队中最小的成员Angela Ha,人小志不小,无论是演唱还是朗诵,无论是中文还是英文,都是一字一句,千锤百炼,精益求精。小小年纪所表现的这种坚韧不拔、持之以恒的吃苦、拼搏精神,格外可贵可爱!

我衷心地期望《晓康歌谣学汉语》给每位老师和学生及广大读者带来一份独特的惊喜和收获,使语言学习成为人生最大的一份快乐和享受!

周晓康
2009 年 1 月 10 日
于洛杉矶—墨尔本的飞机上